The Spirit Within

The Spirit Within
Spiritual Teachings from Gregory Haye

Mick Avery

Edited by **Dr Robyn Sheppard**
and **Sylvie Avery**

Published by Spirit Teaching™, California, U.S.A.

The Spirit Within
Spiritual teachings from Gregory Haye
by Mick Avery

Published by:
SPIRIT TEACHING™, Ltd.
18340 Sonoma Highway
Sonoma, California 95476
www.spirit-teaching.com
(707) 939 9212
(888) 746-6697

All rights reserved. No part of this book may be reproduced or transmitted in any form or by any means, electronic or mechanical, including photocopying, recording or by any information storage and retrieval system, without written permission from the author, except for the inclusion of brief quotations in a review.

Mick and Sylvie Avery assert their right under applicable law to be identified as the authors of this work.

Copyright© 2005 Mick and Sylvie Avery
First Edition
Printed in the United States of America

Publisher's Cataloging-in-Publication

Haye, Gregory (Spirit)
  The spirit within : spiritual teachings of Gregory Haye / [channeled by] Mick Avery ; edited by Sylvie Avery and Robyn Sheppard.
  p. cm.
LCCN 2004107342
ISBN 0-9755599-0-7
  1. Spirit writings. 2. Mediums--United States. 3. Spiritualism--United States. I. Avery, Mick. II. Avery, Sylvie. III. Sheppard, Robyn. IV. Title.

BF1301.H347 2004   133.9'3
                         QBI04-700247

Contents

Foreword	7
Introduction	9
Acknowledgements	13
Chapter 1 – The Spirit Within	15
Chapter 2 – Looking Within	21
Chapter 3 – Death	24
Chapter 4 – Fear and Doubt	27
Chapter 5 – Transition and Progression	33
Chapter 6 – Atonement	41
Chapter 7 – Duty of Care	45
Chapter 8 – Planet Earth	49
Chapter 9 – Love	55
Chapter 10 – Balance and Harmony	59
Chapter 11 – Faith and Truth	65
Chapter 12 – The Spirit Within – Revisited	69
Chapter 13 – The Keys	73
Chapter 14 – Meditation – The Master Key	75
Gregory's closing prayer	77

Let us be together friend
Let me of the physical body
No longer be apart from the spirit
that I am
Let me the spirit that I have become
Grow and move forward in thought
and action
So that what I have become
May bring a realization to others
That they may seek a better
Understanding for themselves

Gregory Haye

Foreword

It has been a privilege and an enjoyable 'labor of love' to have been involved in some small way with the production of this book. Gregory gave specific instructions regarding the publishing of this his first book (and he assures us there will be many more to follow). Specifically, he wanted the price to be kept low in order that as many people as possible would have access to it. He also asked that its content be kept short and simple so as not to intimidate potential readers.

In drawing this material together I have endeavored to present as faithfully as possible the essential essence of Gregory's message, but with Gregory's blessing some editing has taken place. Gregory happily acknowledges that because the following material is taken from the very first information he communicated through Mick, the process, along with his language and sentence structure, is far from perfect. As we felt it important that Gregory's unique style should take precedence over editing to produce 'perfect English' many 'Gregory-isms' appear.

It is regrettable yet inevitable that what the reader misses out on is the congenial and engaging joy, warmth and sincerity that infuse every word when one hears Gregory speak in his own unique way.

On the question of the source of this material, the reader must make up their own mind, but I have absolutely no doubt that Gregory crosses the veil between the spirit and material world to bring us his message. Nor have I any reservations whatsoever about the absolute integrity of Mick Avery through whom Gregory's thoughts are spoken.

Dr Robyn Sheppard

Introduction

When our dear spirit friend Gregory first began to communicate with us, we were naturally interested to find out all we could about his life on the earth plane (as are most people who have the opportunity to speak with him). Gregory tells us that he was born in England, in 1705 (in the county of Norfolk, south-east of the Fens) and that in his earthly life his name was Gregory Haye. He also tells us that he met his physical 'death' as the result of being run over by a coach and horses in the dark, aged only eighteen and a half years old. Gregory was buried near the grounds of Castle Acre Priory in Norfolk.

Gregory's parents were poor and worked as laborers. His mother was French and passed when he was very young. He tells us that whilst he had a hard life he was fortunately taken under the wings of visiting monks at a local priory. From them he received some basic education and particularly loved to write poetry.

Since his physical passing in 1723, Gregory has chosen to serve, and one way he does this within the spirit realms is to help those who have recently passed over onto the next step of their journey. Another part of this service is to communicate via his medium to us on the earth plane, in order to share the benefit of knowledge and wisdom he has gained insight into since his time here on this physical realm of existence. This is not from an elevated position, 'but a different one' as he sees it.

He explained that how, in the spirit realms, he had found it very necessary to build on his scanty education in order to keep abreast with contemporary English language and particularly the modern idiom. In his distinctive soft voice, he shares his teachings and answers our questions in a gentle, modest, non-judgmental, compassionate (and frequently humorous) manner.

The medium through whom Gregory communicates is my husband and partner Mick Avery, who was born in London, England, in 1952. Music played a large part in Mick's early life, both as a performer (he was a musician) and as an audio technician. Mick's mediumship took off dramatically in 1997.

In talking about the early stages of his spiritual awareness, Mick says: "We went to a variety of excellent demonstrations of all forms of mediumship ranging from clairvoyance to physical, where in the latter I just sat and watched in awe of the implications of my own survival. We didn't for one moment consider that any of what we were witnessing would eventually play such an important part in our future lives. I never thought of myself as anything other than just an ordinary bloke and still do, and hopefully always will.

Mick continues: "Before we began sitting together for spirit, Sylvie was sitting in a circle for her own gifts of development. On occasions she would read snatches from the teachings of Silver Birch to me before going to sleep, but apart from that I had little, if any, knowledge of spiritual philosophy. I am so glad of that now, because I realize the information that comes through my trance mediumship has not come from my sub-conscious memory; an explanation often given by some to explain the trance phenomena."

Introduction

After eighteen months of learning to become aware of spirit, Mick's guides and helpers in the spirit realms began to give strong indications that Mick was being prepared for a future in which he would be used as a channel for trance. To say that this came as an enormous shock to Mick and myself would be an understatement. However, having been asked and assured of spirit direction, we then took up this challenge, which changed our lives forever.

Having agreed to serve spirit, it wasn't long before Gregory Haye made himself known to us and he asked me to tape-record all subsequent sittings and transcribe them for the purpose of publication. He said that he represented those minds of clear thinking, of the sentient energy who make up 'The White Cloud Group.' They consist of many hundreds of individuals from various soul groups, who were brought together to educate and instill the love and vibration of harmony and union throughout our world and the universe.

Mick's mediumship has become so finely tuned that he now gives demonstrations to the public all over the world, where people are invited to put questions to Gregory on many diverse topics, and in a perfectly natural way.

There are a number of other communicators that use Mick as a vehicle of expression, including Silver Fox, a Native American Crow Indian from the ancient past. He makes regular contact, giving us beautiful philosophy on natural law and showing in his own special way, how we may go forward in harmony and love.

Mick says: "We never thought for a moment that we might be in any way involved in a book on spirit teachings. Indeed, anything like that was just totally beyond our comprehension, it was always something that 'someone else' did. I had many, many doubts about myself and have fought many an internal battle. There was no way that we ever sought or desired a public life. Just speaking in public was a big one for me, because I really didn't have any confidence in myself; I had a nervous stammer and a very short-term memory. I would have been happy just sitting to try to get in touch with 'who I am,' and hopefully, to also develop my spirit."

A vital aspect of Mick's mediumship today is that of trance healing, where Li Teow Sonicha, a wonderful Chinese healer now in the spirit world, works through him to give healing to both people and animals.

Everyone would agree that Mick is a kind, gentle and unassuming person with a lovely sense of humor. He has made enormous progress with his spiritual development in a relatively short space of time, by sheer dedication and discipline, coupled with his willingness to be used as a channel for spirit.

Whilst I have played a crucial role in recording, editing, hosting the trance demonstrations and conducting workshops with Mick, my own mediumship development has also taken off in new and exciting directions. Our involvement with spirit has made our lives complete, and we regard this relationship as natural and perfectly within everyone's right to grasp and develop for themselves.

In reviewing the amazing journey into mediumship he has taken so far, Mick says: "Through seeking answers to many searching questions that life has thrown up, we feel that we were maneuvered by spirit so that we were in a position to be of service ... and are humbled to do so."

Sylvie Avery

Acknowledgements

We wish to thank and acknowledge all those people, past and present, who have so freely given so much of their time and inspiration to make this publication a reality. In particular our special thanks go to:

Ann and John for their dedication, loving energy, support, and unfailing loyalty to our home circle and to Mick's development and also, Nicki for her friendship and encouragement.

To Robyn for her time and literary skills with proof reading, editing, and her positive enthusiasm!

Simon Warwick-Smith and Cierra Trenery for their professional help and guidance.

Finally, to our friends, both in the physical world and in the spirit world, who have played a part in our life at all stages of our spiritual pathway, we thank you.

__Mick and Sylvie Avery__

The Spirit Within

Welcome friends! The entire journey of man is to enhance the spirit within. If you do not understand this, then the spirit within you cannot elevate you fully to that which you should know. This is why the concept of the spirit within is threaded through every aspect of my communications with you. It is the central key.

Being in touch with the spirit within is a moment-by-moment experience and not just when the occasion suits you, such as in times of doubt, fear and loss. It is greater than that. The spirit within is the essence of God that you are. It is your duty of care to recognize this fact so that the spirit within and you, as an entity, may grow and become more accomplished than it was before you came to the earth plane. It is the purpose of your journey.

First, let us begin by drawing a comparison with something material, which you can relate to. On your physical plane you have a glowing sun in the sky and as you look, it feels warm upon your skin. As it graces your sky, it brightens your life and you feel lighter and happier. This energy-house is only one of so many in your known universe, all boiling and radiating out their energy to the planets surrounding them. This energy source gives to you; it allows you to survive by providing what is necessary to grow food.

Now my friends, there is another sun, one that is not so visible, another energy ball that is within you, which is the real you. It is golden, just like the sun in your sky, but brighter, much, much brighter than anything you could ever imagine is. It is like carrying around an inner blanket of warmth and security, an inner blanket of peace, and like a little cherry that ripens unexpectedly on the tree, it is there for eating. It is there for you all my friends, for the sweetness of love that it gives, a little cherry that you may gain nourishment from. It is a gift of sweetness and light, a gift from the loving hand of the creator.

Open your heart and you will discover it. You will have a lovely surprise and may say: "Oh, it has been there all of the time and I did not know it!"

Rather like waking up four days after Christmas and finding yet another present underneath the tree that you had missed. Except, it is so much better than that, for it is your gift of God that you can recognize within you – however you understand God!

The spirit that is 'you' is an integral part of your nature. Every one has one. Everyone is one. Yet so many people fail to recognize or accept, or believe it to be so. Most think that this is something which is far beyond their reach, some golden figure with wings that has been sent from God to deliver a message to the pious; something that comes to sanction their beliefs, their actions and their whims. However, the spirit is not something that is given. It is not for anyone to give you anything my friends; it has been there all of the time, even since before you were born.

The Spirit Within

You have always had spirit with you, and you have always been spirit. It is impossible for you to be anything else other than spirit. The spirit that you are is a part of the creative life force and energy of the infinite creator. It is your small part of that infinite creator, that we are all a part of – the one divine source of energy and love.

Once you have glimpsed this, you will recognize that there is an energy within you that is far, far different from your own. An energy that is intangible. One that you cannot touch or move, that you cannot see, smell, or pour into a glass. Once you glimpse the energy of your spirit, you will become alive with a different knowing, that you my fellow traveler, will acknowledge and celebrate as truly the perfect hand of God. When you realize that the spirit that is you is undying, it will be the moment when you awaken fully in your understanding of the full extent of love.

It is such a delicate subject as to who and what the spirit is. You may wonder how you might feel it or see it? My friends you have to merely experience it! You will experience perfect harmony, love and light that shines and sparkles within your inner being, and when you discover it, it awakens you from your illusion. Every time you go there friends, every time you visit the little one within you, you will walk with your own angel, the angel that you are. You are all angels, all part of the infinite creator. You are all infinite.

You will find that the fullness of being in touch with the spirit within will make you feel very different deep inside yourself. You see, life is a bit of a comedy of chance really, as to whether you grasp the nettle or not, and as you are well aware, nettles can sting. Therefore, you may wonder if spirit has a sting in its tail. No friends, I assure you that spirit does not have a sting. It yearns to be recognized by you, but it must remain dormant, for the only way it can be released into your life is for you to turn the key yourself ... for you to discover it for yourself.

    Your spirit is very wise and knows that it will mean so much more to you, if it is you who has discovered it. It does what it can to be released from the prison that you confine it to. It yearns to be listened to. To be recognized and allowed to come forth into your life. It waits in the background and sometimes it seizes an opportunity and leaps out as a thought, and it is at these times that you feel inspiration.

    You may wonder where else this inspiration could come from? We may turn on a light within your mind. It is our way of saying: "Hello, we are here!"

    It is sometimes necessary to do this so your thoughts will become more elevated, and having experienced this moment of illumination you will wish to go there again. You will want to re-live the experience, for it makes you wonder where such a thought came from.

    There are so many different ways that we try to awaken you from the slumber of your unknowing in order to expose you to beautiful things. The more you become exposed to these elevated conditions, then the deeper your understanding can grow and we, your friends of the spirit world, do try everything that we can to help you, but sometimes you do not want this help. In fact, much of the time you do not want it, but we help anyway, out of love. For the love that is within the spirit world is endless, it is bountiful and beautiful. So do not despair on those days when you feel you have just had enough of everything. We have not left you. We are always there.

    You may wake up one morning and know you are going to have a pleasant day, because you have worked out some kind of happy agenda. You are going to be doing things you enjoy, so you look forward to it with a lighter heart. See how light you feel? You know you are going to have a good day so you feel light, and that is what spirit is about. It is not about airy-fairy things that you cannot see it is about everyday life that affects you. It is about people inter-reacting. It is about knowing and recognizing the spirit within you. Get to know it, get to love it as part of who you are. After all, you have to spend a long time with yourself.

When you do feel and recognize the spirit that you are, it is like a glorious sun rising between mountains of despair, those mountain ranges of hardship and negativity that have seemed such a hurdle in your life. You will rise in between the mountains of negativity like a phoenix out of the ashes, and the warmth that surrounds you and the warmth you become, exposes the real you within. It will expose the full nature of who and what you are. This is indeed, a glorious moment, when you realize that your spirit is actually a part of you.

The untold joy that is yours is not one that is short lived. That inner light you gain is not one with a short fuse that will fizzle out. With your greater realization and without clouds in front of its pattern, all will see clearly the awakening that has taken place within you. And what do you experience when viewing the world through your awakened awareness? Your surroundings finally become understood and appreciated through your senses.

We know that a lot of the time, mankind is very preoccupied with material concerns, like more money, a bigger car or whatever, but if you had not turned out to be so materialistic what would you have become? Do you not see anything else in your world you would wish to become other than materialistic? Do you not see another option? Do you not see that there is another well to draw from and that the well of materialism will one day run dry? Understand this, my friends – you cannot take any of your possessions with you, they will become just a load of rocks at the bottom of the well.

    The well of the spirit is an infinite source. Although you do not have to, you may be drawn to it; it is your choice. Eventually, you will succumb to it, for it is the thing that your heart cherishes. It is what lets you sing like the little bird that you are, to feel overwhelming love, and it is the very thing that allows you to expand and express yourself in many different ways that you have never dreamt of.

Looking Within

Life exists all around, but you do not perceive it; the ocean, the sky, everything is full of life. For every speck of your world and your universe you see, there are an infinite number of specks you do not see.
 You have two trees in a field; and you may think there is not very much space in between the two trees, but if you look up the space is enormous and goes on for mile after mile. It is infinite. The space between the branches where the birds and bees fly is much larger than the tree itself. The tree only occupies a tiny, tiny space, in relation to the space it does not occupy within its arms. There has to be space, and in that space where solid things are not, there is much life, and in all the space where solid things are (as well as where solid things are not) is where we are.

 Some of you wander aimlessly through life trying to fill a huge void, and it is because you are searching for something, and that something you are seeking is the awareness of the spirit within. Some try to fill this void in many ways, by indulging in excesses; you will try almost anything in your attempts to fill up the gaping wound. Excesses can lead to addictions, addiction of either the mind or the body. You may look for comfort in alcohol or drugs, but friends this void cannot be filled by a physical substance, because what it is lacking is the essence of love. Many of your world have stopped looking and in doing so have sunk lower and lower, until they see no further point in doing so. My friends look within!

Many tell lies of what spirit is, and some say that salvation of the soul can only be available through them. However, you are your own salvation, for you are your own true spirit, and the moment you recognize this fact, the quicker you can move on. You do not need another person in their finery to say to you: "Go this way, for I am the true messenger!"

The world is so vast, spirit is infinite and depth of understanding grows with time. You cannot just leapfrog through life; it is a journey like no other, for it is a journey of love. Furthermore, you can understand a little better when you do not obstruct it with a limited point of view. Speak plainly, so that all may understand. Speak as you find, for what you will find is love and truth. If you speak truth it will sparkle and it will be seen for what it is. All life exists and all life in all forms exist, everywhere you are and everywhere you are not, you only have to look, it is that simple.

When you first came here in your present form, it took many years to understand certain situations, just as it may take you many years to understand that the spirit exists. Yet, man and spirit are one and have always been, and it is the same with animals, trees, insects, birds and flowers. Man is not so complicated. Man makes himself complicated, so that he can be proud and say, "I am" and receive a piece of paper to say so. Yet, the 'I am' may have no understanding of life's pathway, and even then only a pathway to a certain point. Explore with no preconceived ideas and understanding will grow.

We, of the spirit light, are speaking and working with ordinary people who try to make sense of life, and we can be there with just a thought or just an aspect of a thought. It does not matter where you are; it does not matter where on the planet you are. You do not need a building – buildings are for ghosts. For to be and to blend with spirit, you only need spirit and you.

You may wish to go fishing; perhaps you will find your stillness there. You may wish to go for a walk and though not realizing it, it is at those times that we try to bring you in focus. We encourage you to feel the energy and the love in all of the things you look at while on your walk, hoping that this will bring you peace and harmony. However, we will not chase you around. We will not interfere with your life; your life is yours to do with as you wish.

It is possible that man could have infinite wisdom. Everyone, every single entity has a voice within, but so many do not listen and the voice within is everything. We come only to be uplifting. We seek only to bring love and light to your world of darkness. For although you have 'Father Sun' to give you light in your material world, you also have much darkness. You need light from the spirit world, for there is such a need, such a yearning for this light – for this love.

Death

When one upon your side of life faces the loss of a loved-one (a fellow spirit) so many ask: "Why does this happen?" You may wonder, "Is that person lost to me forever?" The answer is no my friends, because you are spirit, you are all eternal. The reason that you come to the earth plane is to learn the lessons that you have been assigned and to move forwards through life. Therefore, at the moment of your passing you simply come back to us.

Your life on earth has given you experience, and as with all life, you have moved on. Even a tree cannot stay the same. It has to spread its seed and move across the face of the earth and wither and die as the spirit of the tree is released. All manner of life has this cycle, and you and I are no different. It is just that you are on one side of life and I am on the other. I have the same love and harmony within me as you have within you.

Your sense of loss when one close to you passes to our side is not necessary my friends. Yes, you mourn the passing, because you feel that you will miss the character and presence of your loved-one who has been linked to you as you both traveled through your lives. The journey of your loved-one may have been short or it may have been long, but it was nothing more than a journey. You are never truly parted from that loved one, because you can reconnect with them at any time, by just a thought. In a second they can be there with their loving arms around you once again, and you will know it, for you can sense it and you can feel it.

To some it can be so very traumatic when they think they have lost a loved one; so unbearable that the grieving goes on for the rest of their life. But, my friends, this serves no purpose, nor is it a service to the spirit who has joined us. I mean this most kindly, that you must try to raise yourselves above this negativity. Raise your vibration, your awareness and your knowledge of the truth. Then the unawareness of the things that you did not understand will become clear, like a fog lifting.

Yes, the physical body falls away, but the spirit who is within, that part which is eternal, remains alive. You cannot die for you are a part of the eternal spirit and your imprint, your memory of whom and what you are will continue on as an aspect of the spirit entity that you are, as you travel back to us. It will travel forward to the group from whence it came and belongs, to the soul group that is that spirit's harbor. To where that spirit's friends and kinsmen are still residing since before the journey to the physical; back to digest and to fully learn the lessons that have been experienced whilst being on the earth plane.

No one leaves anyone. We are all around you still. All of those who have passed are still here; they just enjoy a different form of life. I assure you that the moment you have a memory of a loved one who is in the spirit world, you connect with that spirit, for thought is truly alive and well within spirit life. If at times you feel you need a certain special loved-one with you, then think of them; think with all your heart and they will be there.

Once the understanding is reached that you are spirit form in a physical body, then the fear of the loss becomes more bearable. When you feel the loving energy that was that person drawing close to you like arms around you in an embrace, it can take much of the pain away.

The loss does not exist; it is essentially a man-made institution. It seems that in your society so much revolves around death, around the passing of a spirit, instead of revolving around life. My friends, if those in your world were to actually put more emphasis on life rather than extinguishing life, there would be much greater progress. You destroy both your planet and your fellow man and through wars you send so many to our world before their time, before they have lived out their lives fully. This overwhelms us sometimes, because the spirit of man has so much to learn.

So when someone who is close to you comes home to us, please do not be too heavy-hearted and suffer. The lesson for you is to appreciate and celebrate their life. Yes, celebrate it. Remember every detail with love and then you can move on from the lesson. You must always move forward, to fulfill your own path and destiny, to become that which you deserve. Everyone deserves to move towards becoming a better person, a better spirit and to live in love. Love is a very powerful thing and it is the object of your lesson on your planet. It is the key to your life and the reason why you are living it.

Fear and Doubt

Many people on your side of life live in fear. They live in fear of those around them, they live in fear of what may happen to them and they live in fear of each other. They are fearful of what one man can do to another with apparent impunity and they fear that for this, there will be no justice. Fear plays a very big part in your lives.

You have a huge multi-media system in which you can communicate far across your planet, and all of these communications are capable of bringing you fear. Every action that is taking place within your world is brought much closer to you – it comes into your homes. You can have a war in your living room from another part of the planet. You can have untold disaster visited upon you, sometimes with incredibly graphic detail that you would not normally see in your lifetime.

Believe me my friends, these things can affect you, not only you the person in the physical body, but also you the spirit. They can easily disturb and upset an otherwise possibly quiet and engaging mind. It is no wonder that so many on your side of life experience troubled conditions. How do you sleep at night with all of that going on?

The fear wrought upon you is misrepresented and misplaced, for fear in this form has made you (many of you anyway) complacent, has made you drift from one fear to another, like a drug. Fear then makes you become hardened to reality and think that you are important above everything else – that you are the maker and architect. You even cease to look at labels to see if they are eco-friendly or dolphin friendly.

Fear is big business in your world and I see a world where half of the population is scared witless. Some are scared of their own feelings and some fear that they do not know who they are. Fear appears to be uppermost in the minds of so many and some are even scared of their own shadow. Living your life under the cloud of fear makes a great difference to how you perceive your life my friends. Fear brings the price of living to an unacceptable level.

The world you live in teaches you to fear, and the first and most damaging fear you are taught, is the fear of death. Both your own and those whom you love and on whom you depend. However, you must not hold the fear that those who go before you into our realm are lost to you forever. As I have told you before, it is not goodbye. For although your loved-ones have left your material life, they are still close, they can still be reached, they can still be touched. And they can touch, make no mistake, they can touch you. Be assured that those loved ones are not just a memory, but that they live on within the spheres and realms of the spirit world that is all around you, that is through you, through and within and without everything that exists. That is a very big space. Infinite, as God the creator is infinite.

Please be assured that there is no descent into hell. There is no need for this tragic fear that is held about how the person closest to you has passed. It is not necessary for this recurring vision of their last moments in your arms. Why do you put yourself through so much anguish, pain and anxiety? Rid yourself of the fear that you have lost a loved-one forever, or indeed, that you will one day be lost forever. The fear is unfounded – death does not exist. The material body naturally falls into decay when it has served its purpose, but the real you within the outer shell of the body, does not and cannot die. If that were the case, I could not be here speaking with you now!

Love can conquer everything eventually, so take your fears and put them in the bin. Put on a happy coat when you wake up in the morning, and smile … let your very being be alive. We do not say that you should not watch these programmes on your television, because that reinforces that just living is a fearful experience, but if you choose to play a part in creating fear within yourself, then that is up to you and your free will.

My friends, alongside your fears go your doubts. These are seemingly driven into you when you are a small child and reaffirmed by those around you, which increases your doubt about yourself. So as you grow, doubt and fear go hand in hand. They are both natural, but mankind exacerbates them, prolongs them, and makes doubt and fear far bigger and far more widespread than it needs to be. Yes, you need to have doubt, for if you are on a wrong pathway it helps you to see and determine the truth and to seek the truth. You cannot seek truth without experiencing some fear and doubt.

We understand your frustration when you fail to receive answers to searching questions about life, when those around you do not appear to give you the truth that you seek. But, this is perhaps because it is not theirs to give, as maybe they do not have it either. In addition, it is not for us to say, it is for you to cleave the truth from doubt. Doubt is just a wobbly truth. Doubt was a truth once, but was sent off its course. And as you are a human being in the material world, so you too were truth once, and you have wobbled from one ideology to another.

However, truth comes to you in time and comes in an instant. It may take many of your years, but it still arrives. When it does you will instantly recognize it: "Oh truth, how lovely to see you, do come in." Except, then you may think: "Hmm, is this really the truth?"

You see, there is that little doubt coming in again! Doubt is not serious so long as you do not continue to let it have its way. Like the mind when you meditate, you have to bring it back under your control. Doubt is a condition of lack of control; lack of control of the mind and of your thoughts.

Now, I know for certain that if you do not know of the spirit existence, then you will have many, many doubts and could well believe that the words that come from this one's lips are completely mad. It is simply not your time to see it. Everyone on your side of life needs the truth, desires the truth, but very often when it stares at them and says: "Hello, here I am," they cannot recognize it. Perhaps it disturbs their cherished religious doctrines or previously high held views.

We are not here to criticize mankind's beliefs. You are all on your life journey no matter what religions or beliefs accompany you. Nevertheless, we have observed that very few people really do live by what they preach. Many hide behind these doctrines and banners because they evade the truth. Those in power are well paid I am sure, but when ordinary people see reality, little seeds of doubt will creep in.

We are not here to sow little seeds of doubt in those who have their religious doctrines and beliefs. It is not a matter of belief. Belief is a knowledge that has not yet found truth. It is a little piece of knowledge that has not quite got there. For the very word belief intimates that there is reason for doubt.

So whatever you follow, do not say, "I believe," say, "I know." Have conviction in your heart about what you know to be the truth. There is only truth or lie. There is only truth or negativity. No in-between. No ifs or maybes. Ifs and maybes do not really exist because they are simply a truth not yet born. Moment by moment truths will unfold before you, but if it is not yet your time for them to be revealed, you could call it a belief.

If you seek truth, the real truth, it will come and your doubts will fade and decrease in number. All your niggling little doubts will be gone and each moment of your life will be filled with such a connection with your spirit. You will then learn your lessons you have been encouraged to learn, for hand in hand with your spirit you are able to overcome them, as difficult as they may be.

Remember that walking alongside you, are those of us who are around you at every moment of your life – who love you beyond your conception of love. And these people, the spirit entities who are there with you always, who guard, guide, and keep you safe until it is time to make your transition, will then lead you hand in hand, spirit to spirit, to where you belong.

Everyone on your side of life needs truth, and truth is recognized by each individual at the moment that it is right for them to do so. You cannot force, neither should you, for all have free will. If you do not wish to do so then do not do it. It is simple, it is not complicated. If you wish to seek a higher life then go and do it, no one stops you but yourself. It is in your hands my friends. Your life is in your hands, and we do all we can to guide and protect you. We are the little voice that is within you, but it is part of your journey, so if you wish to proceed, do so.

Transition and Progression

When a person passes from your side of life to our side of life, the actual moment of passing is the same for everyone, but what happens to that spirit light at the point after passing is different. For you see everyone has evolved in a different way, in a different manner. Some may have accomplished all that they had set out to do, whilst others accomplish nothing or maybe various grades in between. Whereas, others may even create a situation in reverse. You can choose to sit in a chair and do nothing but just watch your life roll past, or you can be wholesome and good and still not achieve what your spirit has set out to do.

There are various paths that you may travel on our side as well as yours. For those who are fearful when they pass over, they will find themselves in a world similar to where they have come from. Brighter, but similar: with towns and cities, fields and trees, with birds singing as they do, so they are not frightened by their transitional experience. Others may have had an extreme trauma and may have died in a horrible manner, and these spirits will receive the necessary healing and re-assurance that they need.

For the spirit who has recently passed, this is just a transitional period, which may last a long time in your understanding of time. Therefore, once transferred from your side to our side, the spirit resides where it feels best. Where it feels safe. You see friends, we do not experience time as you do – life just is!

We will speak about progression at this point. You understand that it could be that when you pass over to our side of life, your loved ones who have preceded you might not necessarily be residing upon the same plane. Their experiences may have been different, and although they will be there to greet you when you arrive, at some point they will depart and go their own separate way. For their journey is their own, and after all, you can meet again as you wish.

As you journey the spirit becomes clearer, and like layers, the aspects of your life (plus the knowledge and awareness that you gain) become fixed upon the spirit – that spirit light. It is like adding batteries if you wish; it makes the light brighter, it makes the color change.

Progression of the spirit is such a vast and varied subject. You, as the physical body, are surrounded by an aura that is your energy field, and from that energy field of the inner being we can tell if you are emotionally or physically unwell. Those who are instrumental in healing, who have friends from the higher side of life who work with them in this way, are able to tell when the auric field has picked up any unwanted gifts from fellow travelers. Very often, these blemishes can be attached like a bug clinging on for dear life, and with such healing the aura can be cleansed and made whole. I am sure you do not realize what you pick up from others around you, such as negative thoughts or vibrations from someone else; for we all vibrate.

When you go into meditation you are creating your awareness by opening up your awareness. In the art of doing this you will vibrate at a slightly higher rate to normal, and then the quicker that your vibration gets, the stronger your link with spirit becomes. This quickening is not something that you can say, "If you do this you will find yourself vibrating." It does not work like that. You do not really feel it upon your physical plane necessarily. However, deep within, as you become to realize the spirit light that you are, you become lifted and you are then aware of so much more.

Now, on top of all this you have a soul, and the spirit light is within it. The soul is the vehicle upon which your life imprint is imbedded. Once you have passed, it is the vehicle by which you may, if you wish, 'come back as a message' (as it were) from our world to yours. It is the soul vehicle, by which that imprint is brought. If you look at your being as a whole, your spirit light the perfect infinite part of your being, is at the very centre. The soul is the one that surrounds it and carries the imprint of who you are and what this life has been about. It is that, which is communicating for the purposes of conveying love and understanding, from one side of life to the other. To the loved ones who need encouragement and are prepared to listen, who may acknowledge the existence of the spirit light. For many do not. In fact, most do not.

Once you are upon our spirit side of life you go through your daily business conducted in a kind of silence, and I say a kind of silence, because most of the time we communicate in thought. The time when there are audible sounds (audible in our realm) is when we perhaps have a magnificent orchestra, choirs; whatever music is achieved. Music abounds, there is always plenty of music, and it can often raise the spirits vibrations to ecstatic proportions.

We are well aware that this can stir you also. It can

breathe life and light into your human form. It can open the mind and spirit, because much of this music comes from spirit. It is us trying to open your eyes to us. Still, we communicate in thought most of the time, and if we wish to communicate with one who is higher we have to raise our vibration to do this.

Except, what is higher? Well, once again, when you are in the spirit light, you are learning what you need to learn and continuing to grow as an entity, in order to move forward in your life. Once again you will pass from one existence to another, moving through your life journey, continuing your journey of love and searching for truth and understanding. So you see, you do not just come to the earth plane, die, and then go to the spirit life. It happens again and again elsewhere, as you continue to move through and within the realms of spirit life. As you progress so your light grows – becomes so much brighter, and in a sense, you cease to fit the vehicle that you were, and so you have to move on from it. Hence, your experience of what you call death is actually the gift of eternal life.

We are sympathetic to your many mistakes for they are there for learning, but it is up to all of us individually to take responsibility, so that you do not go on making them. You must strive to do your best, to do your utmost, so that your mistakes will be less frequent and so you will have a happier journey.

Each mistake that you make has a certain knock-on effect, for there are very many other feelings that you also experience, are there not? You feel a failure; you may feel guilt, fear, doubt, shame, and disappointment in yourself. Everyone must make mistakes, and we all do, in all realms of life. We all try not to, but those who do so deliberately, then that is a different matter altogether, because that can have ramifications upon that life for a very long time – in your world or within ours.

For instance, someone on your side of life might begin to take drugs or alcohol. They know that a mistake has been made, but can do nothing about it, so go from one scene to another down a certain road. However, this can be used as an opportunity for learning. Not just for the one who makes the mistake, but also for those who are around them. It is not necessary to personally experience something to learn a lesson. You do not need to have made a mistake in order to know that it exists or what it feels like.

Your progression is important and it includes your errors, for you would not be who you are if you did not or had not made them. They are your experiences, which go with you so you must try not to be so hard upon yourself. Do not beat yourself up, it is not necessary, you do that in a most natural way without making more work. You rush around upon your earth plane in a hive of activity, stress and tension, always thinking: "I must get on!"

Do you really feel that you get anywhere? Your progress is actually quite slow, for you expend a lot of energy in doing things which are not necessary, or which only reap a short-term benefit. Your physical life is a short-term event and none of it (except your memory) can be taken with you.

Once this fact is finally grasped, that you cannot take anything with you, perhaps there might be a different attitude and opinion towards the rest of your life. This, indeed, would be progress in action. For once you become involved with your higher side, with the spirit that is within you, then maybe you may become more involved with and better informed by those spirits who are around you and working with you.

It will be at that time that your progress really begins. That you can actually communicate with those on a different plane vibration. However, first we must learn how to be, how to blend with our self; for we cannot blend with others, before we can blend with ourselves.

I know there are many in your world who do not believe this and will probably feel you are being foolish. Like so many of your earth scientists, they have missed the point. You become like two ships that sail in opposite directions on each side of the sea. You do not see each other. Sometimes, it is good to sail a little closer together, if you can plot a course whereby you meet something or someone who may show you another way, to change your outlook.

Furthermore, the moment that one person feels or says: "no, this could not possibly be," they have ceased to become the intellect that they aspire to be. For in the true world of science, there is no such thing as it is not possible. Everything is possible and it is only your mind that gets in the way.

Yes, it is good to be educated; I do not deny it, for you are raising the whole standard of your community. Nevertheless, there does become a point where you are learning for the sake of it, and not for the pleasure or your growth. Everything throughout the history of your planet has been proved right and then wrong, right and then wrong, and each of these opinions bring about a different chain of events.

As a side issue, because of the fact that you have not designed the machine in which you can detect spirit, you feel that spirit is not there. Yet, one day you can take a normal camera, take a picture and to your surprise, there we are!

You see, we appear when we wish, and it is not for you to say: "Okay, I'll have spirit now – you can come in and speak now," or, "You can go away now." Ultimately, it is our choice.

The progression of the spirit light is everything, for all of us will go on learning through love and through the teachings of the spirit world as they come. You shall learn them one at a time, and through the spirit world you will be impressed as to what to say; it will shape your thinking and your movements in your life. As your understanding grows, you will begin to see that in fact, what you are enjoying is a partnership between you in the physical body and the spirit light within you – the light which you are. It is a partnership between that light and the spirit world, which surrounds you.

Atonement

During your life on the earth plane there are many doorways that you will open. You soon discover that some of them do not lead you to where you wish to be, but if you have already opened the doorway and gone down that path, you cannot go back. This should be a warning that you do not need to continue making the same old mistakes, taking the same old roads. For just around the corner is another opportunity to grow a little wiser, by lifting your thoughts. By accepting who you can become.

Even just a little bud of a thought that you can become a better person, in itself, may soothe the spirit within you, the spirit that wishes to be free. You do have the choice. Choices are all around you and once you open your eyes to one you will see there are many. The more that you learn the more you will lift yourself up, so that you will gain greater insight into what you have done.

Friends, you have all made mistakes, done things that you regret, but for most of you a light will be shown to you at the time of your passing and it will be set there as a goal, so that you may seek to understand your follies. For it is not that you can just disregard whatever you do in this life, on your plane at this moment in time.

It is not the case that once you come back to us in the spirit world you just take off the physical coat, hang it up on a hat-stand and say: "Right here we are then, thank you very much for my time," and leave it there so that you can carry on being a nice shiny spirit!

Oh no, you will have to carry that life with you for some considerable time. It will take you quite a while to look at it. Quite a long time to study its contents, to digest its inner wisdom's – or not!

Still, what happens if you have committed some terrible wrongs? My friends, you will find that you will begin your life in our world at the level at which you left the earth plane. Well then, so what is to become of you? Your punishment is your own, for it is not something that is meted out by the almighty hand of God. It does not work like that. There is no almighty hand but yours. You do these things to yourself by your own hand, by your own thoughts, by your own action, and it is up to you to lift yourself up and move forward.

Some folk who have done ill deeds in their past mistakenly think that they have got away with it. Agreed, they may seem to have. Except, my friends, every single deed that you have done you will have to account for, every moment of it, you will escape nothing. When you find yourself on our side of life you will realize that you have not got away with anything. If you do wrong things against another spirit, you will have to atone for the sequence of events, which have been unleashed. Because it is not just that life that you touch, it is also their loved ones who are around them who have been affected by helplessness or loss from the situation.

How do you atone for these ill deeds? Somewhere there will be a light and it will be so beautiful that you cannot resist but to look at it and see just how beautiful it is, how glorious. It will stay there as a lure – but for some, well, you will not be able to reach it.

My friends, it is not we who pass judgments. You can only judge yourself for what you do and it is yours and yours alone to live with for eternity. You may think the deeds you have done whilst living an earthly life were not so bad.

You may even convince yourself of this and say: "It doesn't matter, no one will notice!" However, one day it will matter and you will notice, because you have done them!

It makes no difference how many times you put those naughty little deeds away and pretend they do not exist, for they do, and not to recognize this is just a mere diversion from seeing the real you. Eventually, they will be explored, they will be dissected and every moment of every single smallest ill that is done will be seen. It will be shone out and depicted for all to see.

On the other hand, once you have fully realized your mistakes, fully understood what your lessons are, all is not lost for you. You are not a damned person, because there is a way in which you can atone for the mistakes that you have made. It will not be easy, but there is a way by which one day you will reach the light. That one day you may feel the full force of love at its greatest, for it favors no one and spreads its arms to all. Every single creature and every person will be touched by love eventually.

You see, there must be a balance. A balance to do with the good deeds you have done versus the not so good. Otherwise, how would anyone learn? I am not saying it is like a naughty boy being kept behind at school day after day, it is not like that. The atonement has to be built and replaced with good deeds; the error must be seen for there to be any kind of redemption. Not that you will go to hell either, for it does not exist in reality, but rather that you must live with your actions and find ways in which to make amends to all those who have been harmed by them.

So go with peace in your heart my friends, and be positive. Be focused on your goal and all those things we have talked about and your path will be brighter, and you may begin to understand just a little of who you are.

Duty of Care

When you were in the spirit life before you came to the earth plane, before you took over and inhabited the physical body that you have, a duty was assigned to you. This was a duty of learning. Your duty was to try, by the end of your earthly life, to be in a better state than when you arrived. Now, this duty is a duty of care of the spirit. A duty to bond with that life form, which is you (be it man or woman) and to be sufficiently still and quiet in order to become fully aware of the spirit light within.

It is also part of your duty of care to look after your physical body. Not only to look after your own body, but also to look after the place where you live, the place where the body resides. As a result of this, your duty of care also includes your immediate and wider surroundings, and that also includes the planet upon which you live. There are many other planets in many other galaxies, where the inhabitants have the same duty of care for their planet as you have for yours. They can make similar mistakes to you (or worse or less) and some may even lose their planet altogether, for some have sunk to such barbarity that it must be taken away.

We, of the spirit light, do not wish for this to happen to you, as we wish you to care for your nursery, your little jewel on which you live. For there are many generations of the spirit light to follow you, and you have to leave your world in the same or better condition than when you arrived, explored and used it.

We observe that in many cases you have ignored your duty of care so that you may benefit more, so you may take a little more than you are due. It is sometimes ingenious how you manage to navigate your way around your duty of care for a material profit. However, it is a hollow profit you see, because it is only profit of a very temporary nature, for as I have said, when you leave you must leave it behind.

While you have been upon your planet and have amassed great fortunes or lofty feelings and ideas of your own worth and they are eventually taken away from you at the point of your passing, what then? Did they really serve you well? No friends, not if you forgot your duty of care to your fellow man, to your fellow spirit traveler and to your own spirit. Remember, that the duty of care to yourself, to the spirit that is within you and to the physical body, must remain uppermost in your mind.

Some on your plane become so totally embroiled with technology that they are forever seeking out new advances regardless (it seems) of whether or not they are of any real significance or lasting benefit to the entire race. To service merely the whims of a few, has wasted much time with things that are not needed, instead of applying the technologies to those things that are.

There has to be a seed of change grow within the entire human race. Not just a few, but everyone must have a change in their attitude to their duty of care. You only have one planet to live on. We, in the spirit world, need it, and other planets like it, for they are important places of learning, learning in a particular way.

It is not just important to the spirit world that you recognize your duty of care to your planet, it is important to the spirit within you as well, because your world is an expression of God the creator. The change that must come cannot be a change in words, but a change in deeds.

Do not let your destiny be one of negativity: "But I cannot do anything to change it – Oh, I am powerless and helpless!"

As many of you know, your planet is a precious living eco-system of life, it is diversely interesting and is magnificent; there are many things that can be changed for the good. Awaken to the truths within you and all of your experiences will add up to a greater awareness of yourself and your world – our world – for we walk hand in hand. We are all the same.

Your time on the earth is borrowed and nothing is yours to keep. Possession is an illusion of the material life you lead. It is nice to be comfortable; to not have fears and worries whilst living on the material plane, but the balance is such that there is an infinitesimally small band of people who are in that position, whilst the rest of the planet struggles to survive. Such people are struggling to survive with nature, forlorn and forgotten by those who have so much. It does not need to be so.

Friends, there is enough food on your entire planet to feed every soul that lives – there is plenty. You do not have to chop down acres and acres of rain forest and plunder the land relentlessly. This is not to say that money or wealth is a bad thing, but the possession that the few hold so dear unto themselves, actually has an effect upon the rest of all life!

Your world is geared to having and not having. Your whole world is geared to the act of jealousy, reward and materialism. Yes, it is pleasant to have nice things and we do not begrudge you being comfortable, everyone can be comfortable. Have a nice car or whatever it is you wish, but is there a point at which those around you fear that they are being misused, or abused perhaps? Does your business involve you in changing the environment in which others live? Do you change the environment of others and give them less than what they are really due?

Just what are the consequences of your wealth and position? Did it really meet your expectations or are you still craving for more money, more power? It is up to you to choose the right paths, to choose your words and to choose your thoughts most carefully. Use your eyes and ears; disseminate fact from fiction, always question and life will unfold before you.

It does not matter what religion you follow, so long as the way in which you walk that pathway is with the best intention, following the duty of care to yourself and those who are around you. Always try to give love, and through this you will receive love.

Planet Earth

(Past Mistakes and Present Responsibilities)

My friends try to think of your earth as just like you. See it as a body of breathing energy, a mass, a life form in itself, but be warned that if not careful, mankind will become like a skin cancer to your planet. You have, for a short time now, become well aware of what damage has been wrought upon your earth by the actions and decisions of the past, but never in the name of love and humanity. The motivation is always to do with position and power, decisions taken by the few that affect the majority.

One of your planets most precious commodities (among many) is water. It can do many things for you and without it you would not be able to exist in your present form. It is regrettable that modern mankind has found it necessary to abuse and pollute that water, which sustains your very life. Since the middle of the eighteenth century, man has gradually been polluting the land and your fresh water sources. The pollutants from the farms and factories have become imbedded in the water table and aquifers that exist below the rock and soil. Unfortunately, it would also appear that although 'Mother Earth' tried to lock up various poisons within herself so they would not harm you, you still dig them out and expose them to elements they would not otherwise have met.

It is not the first time and it will not be the last that we chide you on this subject, for mankind is careless in his quest for more for less. You want more – you pay less! In his greed and blindness, man is not content with merely poisoning the rivers, streams and aquifer, but the very rock which keeps it clean, the rock that acts as a natural filter. It is dug up and taken away and then mixed with other materials, the filter gone forever, so that no matter what you do to it, rain will never again become pure water below the rocks.

Still not content with this, mankind continues this mindlessness and dumps rubbish into the sea. Unpleasant and toxic materials have been dumped into the sea in containers sealed in concrete, which in time will not be able to contain the toxic material. So then you find, my friends that the toxicity levels of the sea will rise and will become dangerous to swim in and may be driven to the shoreline. Not to mention the tragic consequences of the creatures that live in it!

Yes, the sea is a large body of water, but it is not endless, it has its boundaries too. You throw many tons of rubbish into it and think it is like a bottomless pit; ships do it all the time. You even take your household waste and throw it out into the sea. Granted, some of these wastes may be biodegradable and so do no long-term harm, but there are other toxic substances that do, and should never be disposed of in that manner.

The results of these careless actions are your legacy to your children and your children's children, who will be left to try to correct this serious damage. To say that we, in spirit, who can see the repercussions from the poisoning of Mother Earth are concerned, is an understatement.

It is not just the earth's water that we are concerned about. You have recently been experimenting with gases that are extremely dangerous to your planet's environment. Why must you persist upon fabricating and compounding materials that do not exist together naturally and turn them into something new so that they have new properties, only to find that you cannot destroy them? What is the point of that? For it then means that no matter how many of these items, or how many tons of these materials are produced, they will always be there, they will never go away.

We are not here to frighten you about this, but to shake you up, because man has chosen to ignore many of the signs that have been given. Unfortunately, those who are in control of such decisions have too much power and will not listen, for the greed of material wealth looms large within them, and they will not heed the warnings of the many who object to these destructive practices.

Some scientists on your planet have tried to brush off the results of the many environmental follies, and there are many.

My friends, it is not good enough to look to nature and say: "Well, there may have been large volcanic eruptions upon the planet surface, but the amount of damage that we have done is very little because you cannot even see it!"

Throughout your history you have pointed fingers at various times and said: "Oh yes that was a big event that must have been really catastrophic" (perhaps referring to the Ice Age or whatever). Some still say: "What hole in the atmosphere?"

You can see that the vibrant, living, breathing earth on which you live is becoming increasingly unstable the more man carries out his research. It is clear that mankind has a choice. He can go down one path that will halt the destruction or he can go down another, which is for self and profit. If you wish to follow this latter route, then it will be mankind's own nightmare, his own undoing.

  Mankind has a choice and must make a decision. Will you allow the large companies and profiteers to make your decisions for you? How many disasters will it take for you to understand that you cannot rule by greed? You do not have to build out into the sea and end up devastated when lives are lost, when your possessions are destroyed through the violent storms that you have unleashed on your world.
  Yes, it is true that man is an inherently dominant creature who has managed to dominate the animals and the plant life of the earth, but to try to dominate the planet on which you live is another matter. It cannot be controlled and crushed underfoot like the ant. The earth is so much bigger than you are and it is not weak, the earth is very strong – strong enough so that if man takes his abuse too far it will react. You have already seen signs of this, it is happening.
  Friends, I know that we, of the spirit light, have covered this subject many times before and that many other speakers and demonstrators have also, but it has to be said, it cannot be kept quiet. Every voice is a different voice and all of those voices clamoring can make such an awesome sound.

  You see, there is much upon the planet on which you live that can, with an appreciation and sensitivity for the need for environmental balance, be resolved, and most certainly in your lifetime. There are other situations that unfortunately will take considerably longer. Your life needs to be not just about the balance and control within yourself and your immediate living environment, but also about your entire planet, from its surface, through every fiber, to its very heart.

It is just another aspect of living with the harmony of the energy that flows throughout you and your world. The more it is abused the more you will believe it is your right to abuse it and that you are free to do whatever you wish. Thankfully, there are those of you on your side of life who are waking up, but it is already half past eleven in the morning, the sun has been up since five and you still have not got out of bed yet as a human race!

Hence, perhaps you can think of what it is you truly want other than hollow material things, and maybe your sunset will be a little more glorious, with brighter colors you will recognize deep within you. Your journey forward is so important. Do not live with regret, do not hang on to it like some treasured possession; you can let it go as long as you remember the lesson it brought to you. My friends do something about it now, anything, as long as you do not turn your back and walk away. For the moment you do that you are lost from paradise, from the paradise that you can create in the physical world.

There is so much out there that can be done. Think now and decide … what would you wish your fate to be? What would you wish for your children and their children?

Love

Your journey on the earth is all about love and learning who you are. All about learning to love yourself and learning to love your fellow man. Everything and all life that exists on your world is there for you to learn to love and cherish, no matter how long or short your journey. Whether you just wander through life or whether you stop in fields or glades to find sanctuary and rest awhile, you must try to learn to love everything that you come into contact with.

There are many different kinds of love and all are a part of your learning process. We, as your guides and helpers, try to increase your awareness and acceptance of certain facts, so that in the fullness of time you will learn to be better spirit people and consequently for us, there will less to contend with on our side of life, when you make the transition. We already have enough to contend with in trying to help the many millions of those who do not even try to walk the spirit path.

Yes, it is very difficult, so you who are on the path of spirit must try and do your best; a half-hearted attempt is not good enough. It is not sufficient, because it is your responsibility to yourself, to the man, woman, child that you are.

Sometimes, as you go through life you may think: "How can I give that person any more love than I do? You cannot have any more of my love I have used it all up."
How many situations can you think of whereby you sometimes feel you cannot continue to give anymore, that you have had enough. Even within your own family, you may have problems when they are not doing what you feel they should, so you feel that you are running out of love for them.

We are what we generate. If you feel that your love is finite, the implication of this is that it can be measured, that it has a beginning and an end. Therefore, you may act as though there is only so much to go around. Love then becomes precious and coveted, and it is no wonder you do not wish to give your love away.
Yes, love is precious, but it is endless and beautiful beyond what you at this time can imagine. For you will find that the more love you show and give, the more it seems to grow all by itself without you having a hand in it. Suddenly, your love has grown, and even though you may be unaware at the beginning, you begin to grow with it and you are able to give even more.
Friends, if you keep your love wrapped up in a box under the bed, then take it out, take the lid off and let the daylight see it for what it is. If you hold on to your love it will become shriveled and be of little use to you.
Is it not true, that without love you become like an empty shell, becoming a mere shadow of your former self? Perhaps you had happier times as a child, where there was

much laughter and much caring and sharing? The care you were shown was the spark of your love. The care that you were given and the spark that was ignited inside grew and it awakened a part of your spirit. It was unknown to you at the time perhaps, but it did so nonetheless. Your spirit 'is' that love source, but it is not just a human trait, for you as a human being are also an animal; it is merely a different animal coat that you have on.

The love you are capable of, the love that emanates from your spirit light is your seed for the future. So you see, all of you who have experienced such love, who have felt the love that wells deep inside, little did you know that what you were experiencing was from the spirit within.

As I have said before, there are many kinds of love. We speak of love of fellow man or woman, of love of the mind and its thought patterns, of the way that someone is, the love of habit, love of spirit, love of God, love of your world, love of life. It is so important that you understand where your love comes from, that it has no measure and is endless.

Love is generated by acts of giving and receiving, for in the act of giving you receive also. When you give love to the spirit that had need of it, the thanks flow to you in return: "Oh thank you so much – I needed that so much."

There, you have love coming back to you in just one thought. It is like holding a piece of fruit to a monkey. The pleasure is all there in the giving and in the receiving. Your pleasure in the giving is in seeing the delicate outstretched hand of the monkey who is so very trusting. The receiving is obvious, for it gives you so much delight to have given something freely ... and it makes you smile.

How you treat your world, how you respect where and what you are and how you are to your fellows, is how you will judge yourself when the time comes. Therefore, you need to build up your store of love and you can do this on your own, you do not really need anybody else; like the sound of one hand clapping, you can do it. You can hear it, feel it, see it and express it within yourself and within your surroundings. You get no medals for it, but what you get is what you give. You cannot say that your love is more pure than another person's love, that you will only give them so much because their love is not of the same quality as yours.

You think I am joking, but I see there are many on your planet who are like this. The truth will ring very loud upon them. It will be like a thunderstorm, and they will think they have been deaf all of their life, for they did not hear or see or feel what the depth of true love can be.

Love, my friends, is awesome and beautiful, but it is not about blowing away the rain clouds in your life, walking on rose petals or dancing on imaginary paths of sunlight! It is about true reality! Love does not demand that you kneel or sacrifice, but only that you cherish all things and every moment of your life – to be tender and aware of the thoughts and feelings of others. Be aware of the life that exists around you. Give it the nourishment of love and all the thoughtfulness and caring that you have, for your cup will never run out.

Love is bountiful and peace is breathtaking in its magnificence. Like a warm blanket wrapped around you to give you the security that life exists and always will – forever.

Balance and Harmony

Certain events that you are exposed to in your day can sometimes upset your balance and harmony so that you may feel out of kilter. This may not necessarily be an event, which is directly in your life, but it may well be something that has happened elsewhere upon the planet. Whilst mankind is on the whole a loving being, there are also many negative traits within the human personality, so that the wars and battles rage on and men, women and children continue to die in the streets.

All of these negative impulses, thoughts, actions and feelings can actually have an effect upon you, even though they may not be in your immediate surroundings. Perhaps it is an item watched on the television news that serves as a reminder of the brutality in your world and it throws your inner harmony into disarray – or it could be closer to home.

You may find yourself in circumstances, which you feel are completely beyond your control, where you feel powerless to do anything that could possibly lift you out of the situation. You may feel that you are walking a tight rope with no end goal, or perhaps you have lost sight of the goal and feel there is no way out, no end to it all.

Perhaps it is your appearance, for instance your body that you loathe; a body, which seems to bring much misery and may lower every expectation you have of yourself, until you actually have no expectation, until you think you have and are nothing.

However, my friend, you are something and all of these situations have come about because of an imbalance within yourself. What you need is to get in touch with you, with who you are so that the balance can be restored. You need the love within you to come and show itself. Your life here is short; your time (as you understand it) is short, so everyone needs to take responsibility for going within, to discover for themselves that they are much more than the reflection they see in a mirror.

We tend to avoid and skirt around certain problems only then to be faced unexpectedly with others of immense proportions. Life is like that. It places hurdles in your way, which you can either jump over, walk around or stop and examine, to see if there may be some better way. All of these hurdles of life either produce a positive or a negative effect on you. Take care not to avoid them, to leave them unattended when they are small enough to deal with. They may all begin as small hurdles, but if ignored will become larger until they seem insurmountable.

There are many cycles of life, which intertwine, and it is up to you whether you wish to take an upward cycle or a downward cycle. We on the spirit planes of life know that it is possible for you to lift yourself from your despair, from your darkness and from your time of strife. Still, the responsibility is yours alone, to dig deep to find the real you, that fine person within. You need to do this for your own sakes, for it is your life, your journey of discovery.

If you can do this, then your balance and harmony can be restored regardless of what is going on in your world and in your life. So find that little spark, find it and tease it out into the open. Let it play in the sunlight and you will see how beautiful it can be. How positive, how right it is that it should be recognized and set free to guide you in your moments when all seems lost.

Everyone on the physical plane longs for harmony but there are many that never or rarely experience it. They struggle and toil, and instead of meeting their obstacles with positive thought, allow negative energies to overwhelm them. You have all had glimmers of harmony in your lives no matter how fleeting, little moments of delight, which have touched your inner being, through moments of transferred friendship and harmony.

Even just the smallest glimpse of harmony can feel as if you have taken a 'happy pill,' can make you feel like a flower waiting to burst open. Such harmony radiates throughout your being, throughout your auric field, lifting your spirit and your mind out of the trough. Just one little thing can do this, one little touch of harmony experienced by your inner being.

Use this memory my friends, and let this 'positive harmonic propulsion' help you; let it lift you and carry you aboard. Let it stand by your side, for it links you with the harmony that comes when you and love exist with one another. So when the hurdles appear in front of you, take yourself back and remember those glimmers, how at peace you felt, and this will help you through. Remove yourself in your mind to that place of balance and remind yourself that the balance was there at that time because of your positive thoughts and your attitudes.

We, in our world, also work towards understandings and the achievement of peace, truth and love, and when all in balance, all these essences may come together in perfect harmony. It is achievable. We do not ask the impossible, but admittedly, you could say that surely this could only be achieved from our side of life. No, it is within your reach also, but perhaps you do not always give all that you could to achieve this perfect state. There is so much more that is possible. Do not forget that your cup can never dry and that we are always with you to make sure it is forever full.

A good starting point in your quest for balance and harmony is to be aware of not only who and what you are, but also the person next to you. Try to become aware of their vibration and the energy of their life force. This is difficult at first, as you will have your own perceptions, but when you eventually do, you will find that you can relax in their company and be more tolerant, more open and more loving.

Sometimes you might feel that you just do not like a particular person and perhaps the reason is because they have something or are something that you are not. It is up to you to see and appreciate the differences and once you can do this you will probably find many similarities. It is the synchronicity of life that you and they have common similarities, and you may even find that you share similar points of view.

All I am trying to say friends is that to be able to have harmony between people, differences do not matter. Try to be compassionate to those who are less fortunate than you. Give them a hand, not a hand out. Just give them love if you have nothing else to give, for that love will spread and will be a source of great energy, and the more it grows, the more it will improve the lives of others. For some – love is all they wish for.

Yes, your clever technology brings you advances in many areas, but the main frame is really about being able to co-exist with one another in ever-loving harmony. If you do not understand this, you will not move forward. When you come to the spirit side of life, if you have not made any move forward in your earthly life then you must start from a lower level, when you could have been further along and far happier had you learned to live in harmony with all mankind whilst on earth.

In moments of harmony you see everything afresh, as if looking through a new pair of eyes, so that everything becomes so much sharper and clearer. In this moment of clarity, you will feel you have made a giant leap forward and you have of course, but do not forget that your journey of understanding takes place day by day, hour by hour, and minute by minute.

The more you are within balance and harmony, the easier it is for your friends in the world of spirit to blend with you and draw closer. It will be when both our planes of existence can embrace each other more closely, that you will be able to experience the delights of this fusion. In this unique blending between our world and yours we can come closer and closer, so you will feel the upliftment that awareness of the spirit brings. Then it will bring a deeper meaning to your life, and you will be able to dive into the ocean of spirit as frequently as you wish, swimming with every feeling, all anxiety and doubt gone forever.

It does exist. The love and light, peace and serenity is there for all of you. Just reach out. We are here waiting. We are just waiting for you to respond. We wish only that you learn the true purpose of your existence.

So, my friends, with positive thoughts and active energy, you can find the balance, truth and the harmony that your spirit yearns for. It is not for us on the spirit side of life to give this to you, but for you to find it yourself. Each of you must seek it for yourselves. It is up to you to do the best you can – you are your own judge. All you need to do is make a brave try!

Faith and Truth

Faith is a word that is not worth the paper it is written on. It is an excuse for truth. It is there until you find the truth. Faith is only a pathway before you, but it is the gate of truth that you open. Faith does nothing and will hold you back, for it will blind you to the truth.

Anyone can write words on faith. It is easy, for it contains no logic. It contains an untested love. It contains worship. Now, there's another word!

Faith can be a handy instrument, but is rarely used in that way. Faith can be blind, obstinate, even heretical – one man's heresy is another man's freedom. So do you leave your faith in the collection box to be gathered up and brought out when you need it?

Yes, there are many who will hold onto faith as if tied to it by some mysterious rope. Many will hold on to this faith as they would hold onto a tree in a flood.

"Save me faith, save me. Save me from pain. Save me from darkness and the demons and monsters. Save me from death!"

Do not dress your faith up to be more than it is, for faith can lead you blindly, and after you fall into a pit of despair, where is your faith then? "Oh God, how could you do this to me?"

You do it to yourselves everyday and you are very good at it. You are very good at putting yourselves down and then falsely building yourselves up again. I say falsely, because many of you have adopted characteristics, which are not yours. They are not who you are, they are who you wish to be. I wonder whether those of you who have faith live in fear of having to test it. Faith is no good to you, if you fear it being tested!

You will appreciate that learning takes many forms, for all life is learning and it should be approached with absolute glee and yearning. Truth is perfection and truth is knowledge. Now, when I say knowledge, I do not mean history, for history is very often blind, and is only true from the position in which you may be standing. History cannot be regarded as fact or truth, unless you have all the points of view.

Truth cannot be found in a library or written in stone or even within a building, for if it were, you might miss it. It could be hidden from sight. Truth is within the grasp of each of you, for it is hidden within you. Each of you carries the truth within, and it is only a matter of finding the key to unlock it.

Imagine your excitement: "I've got it – I'm on my way – I understand!"

This is what life is about. Understanding the truth for what it is, so it will help shape your destiny. Then like petals on a path it will go before you into the beauty, into the light of truth.

Truth has boundless energy, and once discovered you can never let it go. It has a life of its own and shines its own light. It stands alone like a beacon as all other words fall behind in its wake. For truth illuminates the pathway, not faith. Faith is an old petticoat that may be gathered in and then changed and altered to your requirements. It is not fitting, it is not worthy, not worthy of your commitment to it.

Commitment is a much better word! Commitment to truth, are two linked words that like each other. If you have commitment to truth, then you are on a good, clean, well-swept pathway. It will be a wisely chosen path. Be discerning, maybe even guarded, listening to your inner voice, making sure that you and spirit will walk hand in hand always. Trust only that inner voice ... the one that says: "I know this is the right thing to do."

I hope then your venture will be fruitful, and each obstacle you overcome will in turn help you to overcome your fears and doubts. Then each little mountain that you climb, each rock, each boulder will be a further testament to your commitment to truth. Each truth will be revealed to you one at a time, not quickly, not slowly, but at the pace at which you can absorb it, the pace at which you can handle the truth or sometimes not. It is not faith you need my friends, it is truth!

Your life on the physical plane of existence is a continuous learning process, which you can view as fact or fiction. You gather these views in bundles of thought and gradually learn from them. Each fellow spirit traveler that you encounter has a different story to tell, has a different shade, a slightly altered light to shine. Through this you will learn that there are many journeys and many avenues. Many turnings are possible in this life, and you who are on the physical plane, think the thoughts of humans and not of angels (we call them 'Shining Ones') for you are not yet that evolved, and your thought processes have not become clear.

Yes, you are spirit, so you can become wise. You can become wiser, more loving, more centered and aware of those emotions. You can become more sincere. More whole in the way and manner in which you may impart your knowledge of life, in which you may share your truth to all who would listen. Some of you may simply refuse to acknowledge the truth of what has transpired, because all is manifested upon the mind in a completely different way. Just as an artist can paint a picture with a selection of paints, colors, shades and light, another artist may take the same paint, but seen through different eyes will give you a different picture.

This is why truth is so difficult to find. You can struggle in the dark with it for hours and it will not show its head. It will not be beckoned forth for it is shy and sometimes is not recognized. It may be altered by those who would wish to do so for their own ends, for their own power. As a result, try to have courage upon your journey, for there will be many lions around many corners, and so long as you are not a sheep upon the path of your journey, you will reach its full destination.

We have often said that we will not judge you and we do not. You must try and try again; your understanding is not blind belief, not trust of dogma, but open truth. You will see the untruths coming for you will form a gradual 'knowing' of truth. You will know it when truth presents itself and you will be aware of all there is for you.

There are lessons that you will take, which have been presented by others in many different ways; how you interpret them will determine how you proceed upon your pathway. Each encounter that you make shapes your life, and we, of the spirit light, care about your well-being and progress. For we love you without favor. We love you for who you are, for your great journey with your unfoldment into understanding.

The Spirit Within
(Revisited)

Try to understand that the physical you is just a vehicle and the real you is your spirit, which travels on and forward even after your material body's passing. When you truly accept this, then you will know that you are a part of the great and eternal spirit, that your spirit *is* the eternal spirit, a small section of the whole. So it would follow then, that your God is the eternal spirit and that as you are a part of it, you must be God also. When you can pursue the thought that God is open to and a part of all mankind, it will release you from the idea of a hierarchy of human life.

Give something of yourself, something of, and to the spirit within every day; give this moment freely and unencumbered. Freely, without any thoughts of what you might receive, for it is the act and the will of freely giving that the spirit will be awakened. Try to be in partnership with the spirit within. Try to move your spirit forward and help others around you to see the way in which they may progress. You do not need to point out their shortcomings. You only need to help others to understand that all are spirit first, temporarily housed within a human body form. Take care with your words; unfolding awareness is a gentle process.

Along your spiritual pathways, there will be a lot of turns and we, in our world, try hard to make your paths as pleasant as possible, but without interfering with your free will.

Sometimes, we are able to show you different ways of looking at things, so that you may hear yourself saying: "Oh, I didn't know that!"

As long as you maintain your enquiring minds and your link with spirit, you will move forward. There will be times when you will progress so quickly, you will not realize until you look back, just how far you have come in your thinking.

There will also be times when the progress is very slow, because of your human personalities. There is much conceit and avarice, feelings of self-importance by those who feel superior to others. We try to help, but many are deaf to all but the voices they wish to listen to. We feel great heaviness for these spirits, because they could be so much more uplifted and truly shine. Those who take that path will just have a longer route to run, and many years down the line they will find that they have not gone very far. While they may have made a long journey, they will not actually have progressed.

It is progression at a steady pace that we seek for you all that we pour our love towards. When no progress is made, it may seem to some that the out-pouring of love from our world has been wasted. But of course, love can never be wasted; it is merely that it can take so very long to move just a tiny bit, and then at other times, just a few moments.

The birds and animals know how to acknowledge each new day and acknowledge their place within this great world, within this great life. They dwell, living in harmony with all other life, taking only what is needed.

When you wake each morning, try asking yourself: "What am I prepared to give back to the spirit that I am?"

The Spirit Within (Revisited)

For some of you at this time, there will seem to be no answer, because you, the spirit, have lost touch with the real self. Man must learn to get in touch with the operator ... the operator that is the spirit within. If man the vehicle is not in touch with the operator, it is like trying to drive a car wearing a blindfold. It does not work and you will have accidents.

My friends, you all have a lot to live up to and this knowledge may, just may, change your thoughts. It may also change the way you are to your fellow spirit travelers. For that is what you are, spirit travelers having a human experience, and nothing more. Spirit travelers who retain much of who and what you are from your lifetime on this planet; and what you retain is there for you as a reminder.

Be at one and at peace with yourselves, for there is nothing to trouble you. Do not blindly accept and learn only the things that are given to you. Question and acknowledge, think and connect, experience all that you can and learn all that you can, so you may move forward in the progression of your life.

There will always be new ground to cover, new stones to overturn and new dreams to expose and unfurl in the heart – progressing, regardless of the energy that may be available to you. You can still move forward and you can still fulfill your dreams. It may only be little things, but little things can very often be so precious, so simple and understandable ... a gift from God to you.

The Keys

You have two keys with which to enhance your life. The first key unlocks the inside door, the door to the spirit within – the door that shows you the way to find yourself. Each moment is precious, so you must make the time to sit for yourself; even ten to twenty minutes a day, to reach that golden place within – that place where the real you resides.

The second is the key to access, the key that opens the outside door – the door to the great world that surrounds you. So there are two keys. One is to your inner door and the other key is to your outer door. You see, you have been living in your 'house' all this time, and you did not have any keys!

These two keys are vital for your enhancement and unfoldment so do not forget them, for with practice they will teach you much about the individual that you are. They are necessary to your life, because through them you may unfold your journey, to follow your true destiny.

They enable you to unlock the doors of the reality that exists for you. To lead you into a new expansion of the mind, with a wonderful openness with the spirit that you are. They will help you to move forward in greater trust and harmony, and perhaps make you realize the actual disharmony that you live in.

Once you have really attained harmony, you will never wish for anything else other than to blend with the universal flux of life, with the ebb and flow of energy between the physical plane and the spirit ... because it is all one.

It is good to have the keys to your own home so you may come and go as you wish. So that you may relax into the life you have made for yourself.

Meditation
The
Master Key

In order to find direction, one must first of all find the initial signpost. Firstly, look for a quiet place, the quieter the better, although this is not essential, it does help. After having found this place of quiet, it is advisable to begin to wind down some little time before the event if possible, so that the matters of the physical world in which you live can start to dissipate from your mind. This would be a standard practice for any meditation.

Always open with an invocation or prayer asking for protection of spirit, to illumine the love within you, and for you to become accustomed with your natural and rightful birthright as a fellow spirit traveler who is having a human experience.

In the beginning, the sitter should be comfortable and learn firstly to still the mind. This may seem an impossible task to some, or probably to many.

There are various mechanisms for being able to go within and be silent, but we suggest that if any thoughts come into your mind, just allow them to and then let them go again. Just accept them, but do not take too much notice. You will soon learn to pay them less attention and perhaps stop them in their tracks altogether in the fullness of time and with practice.

The Spirit Within

You will find that over a period of time, the thoughts that come in from the physical world will be less and less. When you first try, you may not get what you think you should be getting, but what you should get – is nothing. Then as you look within (as opposed to looking outside of yourself) very slowly and gently, certain pictures or ideas may become evident within your mind; you will also feel an awareness of new feelings. Gradually, you will find that perhaps colors or sensations about your body will occur. When this happens, learn to breathe gently, rhythmically, and relax. If you stop and think too much about it, your inquisitive mind will want to 'open the box' – try not to be tempted to do this.

You will find friends, that as you open up more and more to this way of being, to the light and the warmth within, the spirit that you are will become unfolded, and your thoughts will expand before your very eyes and within your mind. You will then be able to take on board new understanding and new meaning, for you will see that the world is not as you thought it was. It is blessed, gentle, and loving towards every one of you.

You can learn to relax within this vibration and learn to raise the vibration of life that is within you. Do not sit in meditation for too long at first, 20 minutes is sufficient, but try to allot some time in your day when you may do this. Finish each meditation with a closing prayer or invocation. Always think with utmost peace, love, and harmony, during these times, and perhaps it will begin to change your life. In fact, I know it will!

As you move from one moment of understanding to another and enlighten to the love that is not only within you, but surrounds you, then you will know … life is eternal!

Oh gracious spirit
of every type and form
that may grace my path
and my journey.

Let me see the upliftment
that meeting may bring
let me feel the joy
and energy of love
that flows between us.

Let every step I take
be one of thought and courage
and that every fellow traveler
may know thy name.

May the blessings
of the eternal spirit
shine within us and through us
every right thought and action
an echo of the way in which we wish to be.

Remember every goodness
and every positive kindness
that we may share and show to our fellows
so we may enhance our own journey
into the light.

May all of us seek
the knowledge of truth
and the will to know the difference.

May God as you understand
bless you and keep you.

ORDER FORM

_____ Copies of *The Spirit Within* $7.95   _____

_____ Copies of *Spirit Walks with Gregory* $13.95   _____

_____ Copies of *The Soul Group:*
Its Meaning, Magic and Imagery $14.95   _____

California residents add 7.5% sales tax   _____

Add $2.00 shipping and handling + $1.00 for each additional book   _____

TOTAL   _____

Name _____

Address _____

City _____ State _____ Zip _____

Country _____

Make checks payable and mail to Spirit Teaching, 18340 Sonoma Highway, Sonoma, California 95476 or fax to (707) 938-3515. You can also order by e-mailing this information to spirit-teaching@vom.com, or telephone (707) 939-9212.